THE PERFECT
Picnic
BOOK

THE PERFECT
Picnic
BOOK

LORENZ BOOKS

This edition published by Lorenz Books
27 West 20th Street, New York, NY 10011

LORENZ BOOKS are available for bulk purchase for sales promotion
and for premium use. For details, write or call the sales director,
Lorenz Books, 27 West 20th Street, New York, NY 10011;
(800) 354-9657

Lorenz Books is an imprint of
Anness Publishing Inc.

ISBN 0 7548 0545 X

Publisher: Joanna Lorenz
Editor: Sarah Ainley
Copy Editor: Jenni Fleetwood
Designers: Patrick McLeavey & Jo Brewer
Illustrator: Anna Koska
Photographers: Edward Allwright, James Duncan, Michelle Garrett, Amanda Heywood,
Tim Hill & Debbie Patterson
Recipes: Carla Capalbo, Jacqueline Clark, Carole Clements, Matthew Drennan, Joanna Farrow, Carole Handslip,
Sarah Maxwell, Angela Nilson, Liz Trigg, Steven Wheeler & Elizabeth Wolf-Cohen

Printed and bound in Singapore

© Anness Publishing Limited 1998
Updated © 1999
1 3 5 7 9 10 8 6 4 2

Contents

Introduction

Pack up a picnic and pursue one of life's most delightful pleasures. Despite – or because of – the vagaries of the weather and the other uncertainties associated with eating outside, such as whether the flies will be swarming or the ants preparing for an all-out assault, eating outdoors never fails to be an adventure. Whether you stick a few sandwiches and a couple of apples in a backpack, or spread out a banquet by a babbling brook, there's always something special about eating in the open air.

The Victorians loved a lavish picnic and thought nothing of carrying to the site huge, groaning hampers containing everything from whole joints of roast meat, crab and lobster, salads and breads to elaborate desserts and cakes.

The traditional Victorian picnic feast would include the obligatory cucumber sandwiches followed by cricket and croquet, with games for the children and adults dozing in the warm afternoon sunshine.

The advent of the barbecue pushed picnics into second place for a while, but in recent years there has been a revival, and today picnics are being appreciated more and more as a wonderful way of combining social entertaining with enjoyment of the countryside. Kitchenware companies have been quick to appreciate this, and there is now a vast range of equipment available to the dedicated picnicker. There seems to be a suitable container for every type and shape of food, some with separate compartments for sauces and dressings, and coolers and bags to carry them in. Unbreakable steel thermoses are invaluable for hot and cold drinks; choose a wide-mouthed thermos for soups, to make pouring easier.

While such equipment is by no means essential, it can make a huge difference to the success of your picnic. If you foresee no handy stream to cool your champagne in, pack it in a special insulated bag, and when pouring the champagne, avoid spills by using spiked wineglasses that stick firmly in the ground. Picnic tableware should be bright and colorful to compete with the glories of nature. Have place settings in individual colors for each guest, to make plates and knives more easily identifiable.

A good idea is to pack plenty of cushions and backrests — there's nothing worse than trying to eat a meal when you are horribly uncomfort-able — and pack a couple of garden chairs for older guests. Picnic rugs are pretty, but often too small for a large crowd. An old sheet may be more practical, and will certainly be easier to wash. Spread a few garbage bags under-neath it to keep it dry and clean, then use the bags for taking away your trash when the picnic is over.

Better-insulated containers may have improved food safety, but there's no room for complacency. There's no point in carefully keeping food chilled if you later leave it standing in the sunshine for several hours. Pack any uneaten food away quickly: You can always get it out again.

Always be careful to leave the picnic site as pristine as possible. Make fires only in designated areas, and if you light candles for illumination or to keep insects away, make sure they can't be knocked over.

Most of all, you should sit back, relax and enjoy the delicious food and the company. That's the real enjoyment of eating outside!

Perfect Picnic Fare

BREADS

The original convenience food. Bake your own – it's so simple with active dry yeast – or raid the bakery. Rolls and bagels become sophisticated snacks with interesting fillings, and pita pockets are perfect for holding falafel or salads.

CAKES

It is best to avoid gooey frostings, but fruit cakes and loaves are ideal. Pack them in the pan in which they were baked.

CRUDITÉS

Pack a selection of crisp raw vegetables, cut into slim sticks or strips or broken into florets. Include carrots, radishes, cauliflower, bell peppers of every color, scallions, firm baby button mushrooms and cucumbers. Serve with hummus, taramasalata or tzatziki.

DESSERTS

Light, fresh and pretty – that's the only recipe for the perfect picnic dessert. Avoid anything too fragile, and keep cream-based desserts chilled.

DRESSINGS

Pack oil-based dressings in tightly sealed containers and shake just before adding to salads. Use store-bought mayonnaise for picnics, rather than making your own.

DRINKS

It is easy to underestimate how much people drink in the open air. Take plenty of fruit juices and bottled water, as well as wine and beer for nondrivers, if desired. Use unbreakable thermoses for hot drinks like coffee, tea or hot chocolate.

FRUIT

Fresh berries, packed in baskets (with leaves), look beautiful for a summer picnic.

PASTRIES

Individual pastries, like tarts, turnovers, and filo triangles, are easy to eat, and you can include several different fillings. A large pie makes an impressive centerpiece.

PÂTÉS

A rough country pâté is a good addition to the feast, but must be kept chilled. Avoid chicken liver pâté, which is too perishable.

PIZZAS

For a quick and easy treat, make up a batch of pizza dough and cut out small rounds with cookie cutters. Spread with homemade tomato sauce, add the topping of your choice, then sprinkle with a mixture of grated Cheddar and mozzarella. Bake at 425°F for 15 minutes.

SALADS

Made for outdoor eating, salads can be simple or elaborate. Garnishes, croutons and sprinkles (like toasted nuts or seeds) are easy to pack and turn a simple salad into something special.

SOUPS

Cold soups, such as gazpacho or vichyssoise, are ideal for a hot day, whereas winter looks a shade warmer when viewed over a steaming cup of minestrone. Transport soups in wide-mouthed thermoses and include bowls and spoons.

9

CHECKLIST

- Corkscrew
- Napkins
- Salt and pepper
- Paper towels
- Damp dish towels
- Cutting board
- Serving spoons
- Knives for food preparation
- Sunscreen
- Insect repellent
- Garbage bags

Techniques

PREPARING SALAD LEAVES

Wash and drain the leaves. Break off any tough ribs. Dry tough leaves in a salad spinner; blot delicate leaves with paper towels. Pack the leaves in zip-lock bags, close tightly and store in the refrigerator before packing in a cooler.

MIXING BLUE CHEESE DRESSING

Remove the rind from 3 ounces Stilton and crumble the cheese into a bowl. Beat in ⅔ cup plain yogurt, with 3 tablespoons olive oil and 2 tablespoons lemon juice. Sprinkle with fresh chives. Season well.

MAKING FRENCH DRESSING

Mix 6 tablespoons extra-virgin olive oil and 1 tablespoon white wine vinegar in a screw-top jar. Add 1 teaspoon French mustard and a pinch of superfine sugar. Close the jar tightly and shake well. Shake again before dressing the salad.

MAKING GARLIC CROUTONS

Cut the crusts off 3 slices of day-old bread; slice the bread into small cubes. Heat ¼ cup olive oil in a frying pan and fry the cubes until crisp and golden. Sprinkle with salt and drain on paper towels. Pack in a tightly sealed container.

Simple Sandwich Fillings

AVOCADO & SCALLION

Cut an avocado in half and remove the pit and peel. Mash the flesh until smooth, then beat in 1 chopped scallion and 2 teaspoons lemon juice. Season with a dash of Worcestershire sauce and then add plenty of salt and pepper.

TUNA & TOMATO

Drain a 3-ounce can of tuna. Flake the fish with a fork. Add 2 tablespoons softened butter, 1 tablespoon ketchup and 1 tablespoon mayonnaise. Mix well, then add salt and pepper to taste.

EGG & WATERCRESS

Shell 2 hard-cooked eggs and chop them finely. Add 1/4 cup cream cheese and 2 tablespoons mayonnaise. Mix well, then snip in the tops of a bunch of watercress. Season well with salt and pepper.

ONION WITH SPINACH & CHEESE

Chop an onion and fry in olive oil until golden. Let cool. Layer the onion on whole-wheat rolls with raw spinach leaves and grated Cheddar cheese mixed with a little mayonnaise.

SMOKED SALMON & GRAVLAX SAUCE

Mix 2 tablespoons butter with 1 teaspoon grated lemon zest and spread over 4 slices of rye bread. Cover with 1/4 pound smoked salmon and add a lettuce leaf and a lemon slice. Spoon over 1/4 cup Gravlax Sauce (available at specialty-foods stores) on top. Garnish with fresh dill.

FRANKFURTER & POTATO SALAD

Mix 2/3 cup potato salad with 1/4 cup finely chopped scallions. Use as a sandwich filling with 2 cooked, sliced frankfurters and 2 sliced tomatoes.

PARMA HAM, PESTO & MOZZARELLA

Stir 2 tablespoons pesto into 1/4 cup mayonnaise. Use as a filling for rolls, adding sliced Parma ham, mozzarella cheese and vine tomatoes. Add some shredded fresh basil, if desired.

Finger Food

Fennel & Lavender Tarts

INGREDIENTS

6 ounces shortcrust pastry, thawed if frozen
FILLING
6 tablespoons butter
1 large Spanish onion, finely sliced
1 fennel bulb, trimmed and sliced
2 tablespoons fresh lavender florets or
1 tablespoon dried lavender,
finely chopped
⅔ cup crème fraîche
2 egg yolks
salt and ground black pepper

SERVES 4

1 Roll out the pastry on a lightly floured surface and line four 3-inch individual tart tins. Prick the bottom of each pastry shell with a fork and place in the refrigerator to chill.

2 Preheat the oven to 400°F. Make the filling. Melt the butter in a saucepan and soften the onion and fennel with the lavender over low heat.

3 Line the pastry shells with parchment paper and bake blind for 5 minutes, then remove the paper and bake for 4 more minutes. Lower the oven temperature to 350°F.

4 Mix the crème fraîche and egg yolks in a bowl and add salt and pepper to taste. Divide the onion mixture among the pastry shells, pour the crème fraîche mixture on top and bake for 10–15 minutes, until the filling has set. When cool, pack carefully in a plastic container, adding a few extra lavender flowers for a garnish.

15

Country-style Pork & Leek Pâté

INGREDIENTS

1 tablespoon butter
1 pound leeks, trimmed and sliced
2–3 large garlic cloves, crushed
5 ounces bacon
2¼ pounds lean pork leg, cubed
1½ teaspoons chopped fresh thyme
3 fresh sage leaves, finely chopped
¼ teaspoon ground cumin
¼ teaspoon grated fresh nutmeg
salt and ground black pepper
1 bay leaf, to garnish

SERVES 8–10

16

2 Reserve 2 strips of bacon. Grind the rest with the pork to a coarse paste by pulsing the mixture in small batches in a food processor. Scrape into a bowl  and remove any white stringy bits. Add the leeks, herbs and spices to the bowl, with plenty of salt and pepper. Mix well.

3 Line a 6-cup terrine with parchment paper. Spoon in the pork mixture, pressing it down firmly into the corners. Tap the pan to settle the mixture, smooth the surface and arrange the reserved bacon and the bay leaf on top. Cover tightly with foil.

1 Preheat the oven to 350°F. Melt the butter in a large frying pan. Add the leeks, cover and cook gently for 10 minutes. Stir in the garlic and  cook for 10 more minutes, until the leeks are very soft. Set aside.

4 Place the terrine in a roasting pan and pour in boiling water to come halfway up the sides. Bake for 1¼ hours, then carefully pour out the water. Leaving the terrine in the pan, place a board and weights (cans of fruit or vegetables work well) on top to compress the pâté as it cools. Chill in the refrigerator overnight, then remove the board and weights. Wrap the pâté carefully and transport to the picnic site in a cooler. Serve with large chunks of whole-wheat bread.

Potato & Onion Tortilla

INGREDIENTS

1¼ cups olive oil
6 large potatoes, sliced
2 Spanish onions, sliced
6 eggs
salt and ground black pepper
cherry tomatoes, to serve

SERVES 4

1 Heat the oil in a large frying pan. Stir in the potatoes and onions. Sprinkle with a little salt, cover and cook over low heat for 20 minutes, until soft.

2 Beat the eggs in a large bowl. Using a slotted spoon, lift the potato and onion slices out of the pan and add to the eggs. Season to taste, then carefully pour off all but ¼ cup of the oil remaining in the pan.

3 Heat the oil again. Add the egg mixture and cook for 2–3 minutes, until the base is set. Cover the pan with a plate and carefully invert the tortilla onto it. Slide it back into the pan and cook for 5 more minutes, until it is golden brown on the outside and moist in the middle.

4 Let cool, then wrap in foil and place in a box. Cut into wedges and serve with the cherry tomatoes.

Sun-dried Tomato Bread

INGREDIENTS

3 tablespoons olive oil
1 large onion, finely chopped
1⅔ cups milk
1 tablespoon tomato paste
6 cups all-purpose flour
2 teaspoons salt
¼ cup superfine sugar
¼-ounce package active dried yeast
½ cup drained sun-dried tomatoes in oil,
chopped, plus 3 tablespoons oil
from the jar

MAKES 4 SMALL LOAVES

I Heat the olive oil in a small frying pan and fry the onion for 5 minutes over low heat, until softened. Set the pan aside. In a saucepan, heat the milk until warm. Pour into a bowl and stir in the tomato paste.

2 Sift the flour and salt into a mixing bowl. Stir in the sugar and yeast. Make a well in the center and add the milk mixture, with the contents of the frying pan, the sun-dried tomatoes and their oil. Mix to a soft dough. Knead on a lightly floured surface for 10 minutes, until smooth and elastic.

3 Lightly grease a baking sheet. Shape the dough into four rounds and place on the sheet, leaving plenty of room for rising. Cover with a dish towel and let sit until the dough has doubled in bulk.

4 Preheat the oven to 425°F. Bake the loaves for 30 minutes, until they sound hollow when rapped on the bottom. Cool on a wire rack.

COOK'S TIP
The amount of liquid required to make the dough will depend on the absorbency of the flour. Add half the milk mixture at first, then add more as required.

20

Cheese & Chive Scones

INGREDIENTS

1 cup self-rising white flour
1 cup self-rising whole-wheat flour
½ teaspoon salt
½ cup feta cheese
1 tablespoon finely snipped fresh chives
⅔ cup milk, plus extra for glazing
¼ teaspoon cayenne pepper

MAKES 9

22

1 Preheat the oven to 400°F. Sift the flours and salt into a mixing bowl. Pour in any bran remaining in the sieve. Crumble in the feta cheese and stir it into the dry ingredients. Stir in the chives. Working quickly, mix in enough milk to make a soft dough. Knead the dough lightly.

2 Roll or pat out the dough on a floured surface to a thickness of about ¾ inch. Using a 2½-inch round cutter, cut out about 9 scones.

3 Transfer the scones to a nonstick baking sheet. Brush with milk, then sprinkle with cayenne pepper. Bake for 15 minutes, until golden brown. Let

the scones cool on a wire rack, then pack in a tin. Serve with butter, or with a spread made by mixing cream cheese and finely snipped fresh chives.

Dill & Potato Cakes

INGREDIENTS

2 cups self-rising flour
pinch of salt
3 tablespoons butter, softened
1 tablespoon finely chopped fresh dill
1 cup mashed potatoes, freshly made
2–3 tablespoons milk

MAKES 10

1 Preheat the oven to 450°F. Grease a large baking sheet. Sift the flour and salt into a mixing bowl. Add the butter and dill. Mix in the mashed potatoes, with enough milk to make a soft, pliable dough.

2 Roll out the dough on a lightly floured surface. Cut into 10 neat rounds, using a 3-inch cutter. Place the rounds on the prepared baking sheet and bake for 25 minutes, until risen and golden.

3 Let the cakes cool on a wire rack, then pack them in a tin. For a special picnic treat, serve with crème fraîche and smoked salmon.

VARIATION

Cheese & Herb Potato Cakes: Stir about ½ cup crumbled blue cheese into the mashed potato mixture, and substitute fresh chives for the dill. Use 3 tablespoons sour cream instead of the butter.

23

Salad Days

Green Bean Salad

INGREDIENTS

6 ounces cherry tomatoes, halved
1 teaspoon sugar
1 pound green beans, trimmed
6 ounces feta cheese, cut into small wedges
salt and ground black pepper
DRESSING
3 tablespoons white wine vinegar
1/4 teaspoon Dijon mustard
2 garlic cloves, crushed
6 tablespoons olive oil

SERVES 6

1 Preheat the oven to 450°F. Put the cherry tomatoes on a baking sheet with the cut sides up. Sprinkle with the sugar and add salt and pepper to taste. Bake the tomatoes in the preheated oven for about 20 minutes, then let them cool.

2 Bring a saucepan of lightly salted water to a boil. Add the green beans and cook for about 10 minutes. Meanwhile, make the dressing. Mix the white wine vinegar, mustard and garlic in a bowl. Gradually whisk in the oil and add salt and pepper to taste.

3 Drain the cooked beans, transfer them to a bowl and immediately pour the dressing over them. Toss well to ensure that the dressing is evenly distributed.

4 When the beans have cooled, stir in the roasted cherry tomatoes and the wedges of feta cheese. Pack the salad in a sealed plastic container and keep in the refrigerator before transporting to the picnic site in a cooler.

27

Potato Salad with Sausage

INGREDIENTS

1 pound small waxy potatoes
2–3 tablespoons dry white wine
2 shallots, finely chopped
1 tablespoon chopped fresh parsley
1 tablespoon chopped fresh tarragon
6 ounces cooked garlic sausage,
such as kielbasa, sliced
parsley sprig, to garnish
DRESSING
1 tablespoon tarragon vinegar
2 teaspoons Dijon mustard
5 tablespoons olive oil
salt and ground black pepper

SERVES 4

1 Put the potatoes in a saucepan with lightly salted cold water to cover. Bring to a boil, lower the heat and simmer for 10–15 minutes, until they are tender.

2 Drain the potatoes, refresh them under cold running water and drain again. Peel the potatoes if desired, or leave in their skins. Cut into ¼-inch slices, place in a bowl and sprinkle with the wine and shallots.

3 Make the dressing. Mix the vinegar and mustard in a bowl. Gradually whisk in the oil, and season to taste. Pour the dressing over the potato mixture.

4 Sprinkle the chopped parsley and tarragon on the salad, and add the sausage slices. Toss lightly to mix. Season with salt and pepper. Pack in a plastic container and serve at room temperature, garnished with a fresh parsley sprig.

VARIATION

If desired, leave out the sausage and serve the potato salad without it.

Frisée Salad with Bacon

INGREDIENTS

1 head frisée lettuce, separated into leaves
3 tablespoons extra-virgin olive oil
6 ounces slab bacon, diced
1 thick slice white bread, crust removed, diced
DRESSING
1 garlic clove, bruised
1 tablespoon red wine vinegar
2 teaspoons Dijon mustard
3 tablespoons olive oil
salt and ground black pepper

SERVES 4

1 Tear the lettuce leaves into bite-size pieces and place in a bowl. Wash, dry and store in a plastic bag in the salad compartment of the refrigerator.

2 Heat 1 tablespoon of the oil in a frying pan. Add the bacon and fry over medium heat until well browned, stirring occasionally. Using a slotted spoon, lift out the bacon pieces and drain on paper towels.

3 Add another 2 tablespoons oil to the pan. When hot, fry the bread cubes, turning frequently, until evenly browned. Remove the croutons with a slotted spoon and drain them on paper towels. When cold, pack the croutons and bacon in separate plastic containers.

4 Make the dressing. Mix the garlic, vinegar, mustard and oil in a tightly sealed jar. Season with salt and pepper to taste.

5 Pack the lettuce, bacon, croutons and dressing separately. When ready to serve, transfer the lettuce to a salad bowl and add the bacon and croutons. Shake the dressing well and pour it over the salad. Toss quickly, making sure the salad leaves are evenly covered, and serve.

COOK'S TIP

For serving at home, make this a warm salad.
Fry the croutons first, then the bacon cubes.
Drain them on paper towels. Add the garlic,
vinegar, mustard and remaining oil to the
frying pan. Whisk over the heat until warm,
then pour over the lettuce and toss lightly.
To serve, sprinkle the lettuce with the
fried bacon and croutons.

Spanish Potatoes

INGREDIENTS

1½ pounds small new potatoes
2 garlic cloves, sliced
1 small dried red chili, crumbled
½ teaspoon ground cumin
2 teaspoons mild paprika
2 tablespoons red wine vinegar
5 tablespoons olive oil
1 red or green bell pepper, seeded and sliced
coarse sea salt, to serve

SERVES 4

32

1 Put the potatoes in a saucepan with lightly salted cold water to cover. Bring to a boil, lower the heat and simmer for 15 minutes, until they are tender.

2 Drain the potatoes, refresh them under cold running water and drain again. Peel the potatoes if desired, or leave them in their skins. Cut into chunks.

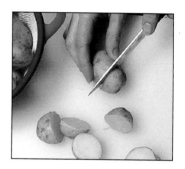

3 Put the sliced garlic and chili in a mortar. Crush with a pestle, then add the ground cumin, paprika and red wine vinegar and mix to form a paste.

4 Heat the oil in a large frying pan and fry the potatoes until golden, turning them often. Add the bell pepper slices and cook for 1 minute, then stir in the garlic paste. Cook, stirring, for 2 minutes. Transfer the spiced potatoes to a bowl and let cool. Cover the bowl securely for packing and grind sea salt over the potatoes just before serving.

Swiss Cheese Salad

INGREDIENTS

2 skinless, boneless chicken breasts
1 1/4 cups chicken stock
1/2 pound Gruyère cheese
1/2 pound thickly sliced cooked ham
1 head green leaf lettuce
1 head Boston lettuce
1 bunch watercress
3 celery sticks, sliced
1/4 cup sesame seeds, toasted
2 Granny Smith apples
DRESSING
5 tablespoons sunflower oil
1 teaspoon sesame oil
3 tablespoons lemon juice
2 teaspoons chopped fresh mint
3 drops of Tabasco sauce

SERVES 4

1 Put the chicken breasts in a saucepan. Pour in the stock and bring to the simmering point. Simmer for 15 minutes, or until the chicken is just cooked. Drain, reserving the stock for another recipe. Cool the chicken quickly in the refrigerator.

2 Make the dressing by mixing all the ingredients in a tightly sealed jar. Cut the chicken, cheese and ham into fine strips. Put in a plastic container, moisten with a little of the dressing and chill in the refrigerator until needed.

3 Wash and dry the lettuce leaves. Pack them, with the celery, in a loosely closed plastic bag in a cooler. Add the container of cheese and meat and pack the sesame seeds and apples separately, with the dressing. Dress the leaves and assemble the salad on individual plates at the picnic site, slicing the apples and adding them at the last minute.

Stuffed Bell Peppers

INGREDIENTS

6 bell peppers, any color
¼ cup olive oil, plus extra for drizzling
1 large onion, finely chopped
3 drained canned anchovy fillets, chopped
2 garlic cloves, crushed
3 tomatoes, peeled and diced
¼ cup white wine
4 cups cooked rice (about 1 cup raw)
3 tablespoons finely chopped fresh parsley
⅔ cup diced mozzarella cheese
6 tablespoons grated Parmesan cheese
salt and ground black pepper
flat-leaf parsley, to garnish

SERVES 6

1 Preheat the oven to 375°F. Cut the tops off the bell peppers and remove the cores and seeds. Trim the bottoms, if necessary, so that the peppers stand level. Bring a saucepan of lightly salted water to a boil, add the bell peppers and blanch for 3–4 minutes. Lift out with a slotted spoon and dry inside and out with paper towels.

2 Heat the olive oil in a large frying pan and fry the chopped onion for about 5 minutes, until softened. Stir in the chopped anchovy fillets, garlic, tomatoes and white wine. Cook, stirring occasionally, for 5 minutes.

3 Remove the onion mixture from the heat. Stir the cooked rice, parsley, mozzarella and two-thirds of the Parmesan into the onion mixture. Season with salt  and pepper to taste. Sprinkle the pepper cavities with salt and pepper, then stuff with the filling.

4 Stand the peppers upright in a shallow baking dish that will just hold them comfortably. Top with the remaining Parmesan and drizzle with a little olive oil. Pour in enough water to come ½ inch up the sides of the peppers.

5 Bake the peppers in the preheated oven for about 25 minutes, then let them cool to room temperature. Transport the peppers to the picnic site in the dish in which they were baked, using balls of crumpled foil to keep them upright. Garnish each of the peppers with a sprig of flat-leaf parsley before serving.

34

Main Attractions

Chicken & Apricot Filo Pie

INGREDIENTS

½ cup bulgur
½ cup boiling water
6 tablespoons butter
1 onion, chopped
2 cups ground chicken
¼ cup dried apricots,
finely chopped
¼ cup blanched almonds, chopped
1 teaspoon ground cinnamon
½ teaspoon ground allspice
¼ cup plain yogurt
1 tablespoon snipped fresh chives
2 tablespoons chopped fresh parsley
6 large sheets filo pastry
salt and ground black pepper, to taste
halved fresh chives, to garnish

SERVES 6

1 Preheat the oven to 400°F. Soak the bulgur in boiling water for 10 minutes, until the water is absorbed. Drain and squeeze dry.

2 Heat 2 tablespoons of the butter in a frying pan. Fry the onion and chicken gently until golden. Stir in the apricots, almonds and bulgur; cook for 2 more minutes. Remove from the heat and stir in the spices, yogurt, fresh herbs and seasoning.

3 Melt the remaining butter. Cut the filo into 10-inch rounds. Layer three rounds in a 9-inch tart pan, brushing each of the layers with melted butter. Spoon in the chicken mixture, then crumple the remaining filo rounds, brush each one with butter, and place them on top of the pie.

4 Brush on any remaining butter and bake for about 30 minutes, until the crust is golden and crisp. When the pan has cooled, pack it carefully in a rigid box (filo is fragile). Serve the pie in wedges, garnished with fresh chives.

37

Stuffed Turkey Breast with Lemon

INGREDIENTS

1 turkey breast (1½ pounds), in one piece
1 carrot, cut into matchsticks
1 zucchini, cut into matchsticks
3 ounces cooked ham, cut into matchsticks
2 thick slices white bread, crusts removed,
soaked in a little milk to soften
10 pitted green olives, finely chopped
1 large garlic clove, crushed
¼ cup chopped fresh parsley
¼ cup finely shredded fresh basil
1 egg, lightly beaten
¼ teaspoon grated lemon rind
2 tablespoons grated Parmesan cheese
¼ cup olive oil
1 cup warm chicken stock
½ lemon, cut into thin wedges
salt and ground black pepper

SERVES 4–5

1 Remove any bones, skin and fat from the turkey. Cut partway through the breast so the halves can be opened out like a book. Pound the meat to obtain one large piece of even thickness.

2 Preheat the oven to 400°F. Blanch the carrot and zucchini sticks in a pan of boiling water for 2 minutes, then drain and mix with the ham.

3 Squeeze the bread dry, place it in a mixing bowl and break it up with a fork. Add the olives, garlic, herbs, egg, lemon rind and Parmesan cheese. Season with salt and pepper and mix well.

4 Spread the bread mixture on the meat, leaving a narrow border around the outside. Arrange the vegetable and ham matchsticks on top, then roll the turkey breast up and tie it with a piece of string.

5 Heat the olive oil in a flameproof casserole and brown the turkey roll. Add the stock and lemon wedges, cover the dish and bake for 15 minutes. Remove the lid and take out the lemon wedges. Bake, uncovered, for 30 more minutes, basting occasionally, until the roll is fully cooked. Cool quickly in the refrigerator. Wrap the turkey roll in two layers of foil and slice at the picnic site. Serve with green salad or a lemon mayonnaise.

38

Cod Plaki

INGREDIENTS

1¼ cups olive oil
2 onions, thinly sliced
3 beefsteak tomatoes, roughly chopped
3 garlic cloves, thinly sliced
1 teaspoon sugar
1 teaspoon chopped fresh dill
1 teaspoon chopped fresh mint
1 teaspoon chopped fresh celery leaves
1 tablespoon chopped fresh parsley
1¼ cups water
6 cod steaks
juice of 1 lemon
salt and ground black pepper
fresh herbs, to garnish

SERVES 6

2 Place the fish steaks on top of the mixture and cook gently for 10–12 minutes, or until the fish is just cooked. Pour the lemon juice over the fish. Lift

out the cod steaks with a slotted spoon and arrange them in a tightly-sealed plastic container. Spoon the sauce on top and cool quickly in the refrigerator. Pack in a cooler. Garnish with fresh herbs to serve.

1 Heat the oil in a frying pan and fry the onions until golden. Add the tomatoes, garlic, sugar and chopped herbs. Cook for 2 more minutes, then pour in the

water. Add seasoning and simmer for 25 minutes, or until the liquid has reduced by one-third.

Sweet Potato Roulade

INGREDIENTS

1 pound sweet potatoes, freshly boiled
12 allspice berries, crushed
4 eggs, separated
½ cup grated Edam or
Cheddar cheese
salt and ground black pepper
1 tablespoon sesame seeds
FILLING
1 cup low-fat cream cheese
5 tablespoons plain yogurt
6–8 scallions, thinly sliced
2 tablespoons chopped Brazil nuts, roasted

SERVES 6

1 Preheat the oven to 400°F. Grease a 13 x 10-inch jelly roll pan and line with parchment paper. Make the filling by mixing the cream cheese, yogurt, scallions and nuts in a bowl. Cover the mixture and keep in the refrigerator until needed.

2 Chop the sweet potato roughly and put it in a food processor with the allspice. Pulse until just smooth, then spoon into a bowl and stir in the egg yolks, cheese and salt and pepper to taste.

3 Whisk the egg whites to stiff peaks. Lightly stir one-third of the whites into the sweet potato mixture to lighten it, then fold in the rest. Spoon the mixture into the prepared pan, level the surface and bake for 10–15 minutes, until firm to the touch.

4 Have ready a sheet of parchment paper on a clean dish towel. Sprinkle the paper with the sesame seeds, then carefully invert the cooked sponge onto it. Trim the edges, roll up the sponge and let cool. Unroll, spread with the filling and roll up again. Pack in a rigid box and slice at the picnic site. Serve with salad leaves.

41

Mediterranean Quiche

INGREDIENTS

2 cups all-purpose flour
pinch of salt
pinch mustard powder
½ cup chilled butter, cubed
½ cup grated Gruyère cheese
2 tablespoons mild French mustard
FILLING
1 can (2 ounces) anchovy fillets, drained
¼ cup milk
3 tablespoons olive oil
2 large Spanish onions, sliced
1 red bell pepper, seeded and sliced
3 egg yolks
1½ cups heavy cream
1 garlic clove, crushed
*1½ cups grated aged
Cheddar cheese*
2 large tomatoes, thickly sliced
salt and ground black pepper
shredded fresh basil, to garnish

SERVES 10–12

1 Mix the flour, salt and mustard powder in a food processor. Add the butter and pulse the mixture until it resembles bread crumbs. Add the cheese and process briefly. With the motor running, add ice water until the mixture forms a ball. Wrap the dough in plastic wrap and chill for 30 minutes.

2 Preheat the oven to 400°F. Make the filling. Soak the anchovies in the milk for 20 minutes. Heat the oil in a frying pan and fry the onions and red bell pepper until soft. In a bowl, beat the egg yolks, cream, garlic and Cheddar cheese with plenty of salt and pepper.

3 Roll out the pastry on a lightly floured surface and use it to line a 9-inch tart pan. Spread the mustard on the pastry shell. Arrange the tomatoes in a layer on the bottom, add the onion mixture and arrange the drained anchovies on top.

4 Pour the egg mixture over the filling and bake for 20–25 minutes. Lower the oven temperature to 350°F and bake for 25 more minutes. Let cool, wrap the pan in foil and pack it in a rigid box. Serve the quiche in slices, garnished with the fresh basil.

Broccoli & Chestnut Terrine

INGREDIENTS

1 pound broccoli, cut into small florets
½ pound cooked chestnuts, roughly chopped
1 cup fresh whole-wheat bread crumbs
¼ cup plain yogurt
2 tablespoons grated Parmesan cheese
2 eggs, beaten
salt and ground black pepper

SERVES 4–6

1 Preheat the oven to 350°F. Line a 2-pound loaf pan with parchment paper. Blanch or steam the broccoli for 3–4 minutes, until just tender. Drain well. Set aside about a quarter of the smallest florets and chop the rest finely.

2 In a large bowl, mix the chopped chestnuts, bread crumbs, yogurt and Parmesan cheese. Stir in salt and pepper to taste, then fold in the chopped broccoli florets and beaten eggs.

3 Gently fold the reserved florets into the mixture. Spoon into the prepared loaf pan and level the surface with the back of a wooden spoon.

4 Place the pan in a roasting pan and pour in boiling water to come halfway up the sides. Bake for 25 minutes. Cool quickly in the refrigerator, wrap the tin in foil and pack it in a box. At the picnic site, turn it out onto a cutting board. Cut into slices and serve with salad leaves and new potatoes, if desired.

COOK'S TIP
For an unbeatable taste sensation, serve the terrine with Spanish Potatoes and fresh cherry tomatoes.

Country Pie

INGREDIENTS

2 pounds puff pastry, thawed if frozen
beaten egg, to glaze
FILLING
1 small duck
1 small chicken
¾ pound salt pork, ground
1 egg, lightly beaten
2 shallots, finely chopped
½ teaspoon ground cinnamon
½ teaspoon grated fresh nutmeg
1 teaspoon Worcestershire sauce
finely grated rind of 1 lemon
salt and ground black pepper
¾ cup red wine
2½ cups well-flavored stock
1 tablespoon gelatin
HOT WATER PASTRY
6 cups flour
8 ounces vegetable shortening (in stick form,
chilled), cubed
1¼ cups water
beaten egg, to glaze

SERVES 12

1 Make the filling. Dice the poultry breasts and set them aside. Trim the carcasses, and mix the meat with the pork. Add the beaten egg, shallots, spices, Worcestershire sauce and lemon rind. Season well. Pour in all but 1 tablespoon wine. Marinate for 15 minutes.

2 Make the pastry. Sift the flour into a bowl. Bring the fat and water to a boil, pour the mixture onto the flour and mix quickly into a dough. Cool slightly, then knead. Keep warm, covered with a cloth.

3 Preheat the oven to 400°F. Roll out the pastry on a lightly floured surface. Use two-thirds of the pastry to line a greased 10-inch cake pan; let a little pastry hang over the top. Fill with alternate layers of pork mixture and diced poultry and salt pork. Make a lid with the remaining pastry and seal well. Cut two large slits in the lid and add pastry decorations.

4 Bake for 20 minutes, glaze with egg and lower the oven temperature to 350°F. Cover the pie with foil and bake for 1 more hour.

5 Degrease the stock. Pour the stock into a pan, heat it and whisk in the gelatin until no lumps are left. Insert a funnel in the pie and pour in the stock. Chill the pie in the refrigerator for 24 hours before wrapping and packing. Cut the pie into thick wedges to serve.

Wild Mushroom Pie

INGREDIENTS

1 pound puff pastry, thawed if frozen
beaten egg, to glaze
FILLING
⅔ cup butter
2 shallots, finely chopped
2 garlic cloves, crushed
4 cups mixed wild mushrooms, sliced
3 tablespoons chopped fresh parsley
2 tablespoons heavy cream
salt and ground black pepper

SERVES 6

1 Make the filling. Melt 4 tablespoons of the butter in a large saucepan. Gently fry the chopped shallots and crushed garlic cloves over low heat for about 5 minutes, until softened but not browned.

2 Add the remaining butter to the pan. When it has melted, stir in the mushrooms and cook over low heat for 35–40 minutes. Pour off the excess liquid and stir in the chopped parsley and heavy cream, adding salt and ground black pepper to taste. Let the mixture cool.

3 Preheat the oven to 425°F. Roll out half the pastry on a lightly floured surface. Using a plate as a guide, cut out a 9-inch round. Place the round on a baking sheet and pile the filling in the center. Roll out the rest of the pastry and cut a slightly larger round to cover the base and filling. Drape the pastry over the rolling pin and lay it over the filling, then firmly press the pastry edges together to seal.

4 Brush the top of the pie with beaten egg to glaze and decorate with pastry trimmings. Cut three slits in the top of the crust. Bake for 45 minutes or until the pastry has risen and is golden. Turn the pie out onto a wire rack and let cool completely, then wrap it in foil and transport to the picnic site in a rigid box. Cut the pie into thick wedges to serve.

48

Sweet Treats

Apple Crumble Cake

INGREDIENTS

CRUMBLE TOPPING
¾ cup self-rising flour
½ teaspoon ground cinnamon
3 tablespoons butter
2 tablespoons superfine sugar
FRUIT BASE
¼ pound butter, softened
6 tablespoons superfine sugar
1 egg, beaten
1 cup self-rising flour, sifted
2 apples, peeled, cored and sliced
⅓ cup golden raisins

SERVES 8–10

1 Preheat the oven to 350°F. Grease a deep 7-inch tart pan, line the base with waxed paper and grease the paper.

2 Make the topping. Sift the flour and cinnamon into a large mixing bowl. Rub the butter into the flour until it resembles bread crumbs, then stir in the sugar. Set aside.

3 Make the fruit base. Place the butter, sugar, egg and flour in a bowl and beat for 1–2 minutes, until smooth. Spoon into the prepared pan.

4 Combine the apple slices (reserving some for decorating) and golden raisins and spread them evenly over the top. Sprinkle with the topping. Bake in the center of the oven for about 1 hour. Cool in the pan for 10 minutes before turning out onto a wire rack and peeling off the paper.

5 Decorate the cake with slices of red apple and sprinkle with superfine sugar and a pinch of ground cinnamon. Transport the cake to the picnic in a tin. Serve in thick slices with cream, if desired.

51

Savarin with Summer Fruit

INGRÈDIENTS

½ cup butter, softened
2½ cups all-purpose flour
¼ ounce package active dried yeast
¼ cup superfine sugar
4 eggs, beaten
¼ cup warm water
1 teaspoon vanilla extract
1 pound fresh raspberries or
strawberries, hulled
mint leaves, to decorate
whipped cream, to serve
SYRUP
1 cup superfine sugar
2½ cups water
6 tablespoons red currant jelly
3 tablespoons kirsch (optional)

SERVES 4–6

1 Using 1 tablespoon of the butter, generously grease a 9-inch ring mold. Put the flour, yeast and sugar in a food processor and pulse to mix. With the motor running, add the beaten eggs, water and vanilla through the feeder tube. Process to a soft dough, scraping down the sides of the processor as needed, then add the remaining butter and pulse about 10 times to incorporate it.

2 Place the dough in evenly spaced spoonfuls around the ring mold. Cover the mold and leave the dough to rise until it has doubled in bulk. Preheat the oven to 400°F.

3 Place the ring mold in the oven and immediately turn the heat down to 350°F. Bake for 25 minutes, until golden brown and springy to the touch. Cool on a wire rack.

4 Make the syrup by heating the sugar, water and two-thirds of the red currant jelly in a pan. Stir until smooth, then boil for 3 minutes. Cool slightly, then add the kirsch, if using. Stir 2 tablespoons of the syrup into the reserved red currant jelly until it dissolves, to make a glaze. Set aside.

5 Place the warm cake on a wire rack over a baking sheet. Spoon the syrup over it repeatedly until absorbed, then carefully place the cake in a shallow serving dish and pour on any remaining syrup. Brush the red currant glaze on the top. Cover and transport very carefully. Pack the berries, cream and mint leaves separately. At the picnic, fill the center with berries. Decorate, then serve with cream.

Raspberry Crumble Muffins

INGREDIENTS

1½ cups all-purpose flour
2 teaspoons baking powder
pinch of salt
¼ cup superfine sugar
¼ cup light brown sugar
1 teaspoon ground cinnamon
½ cup butter, melted
1 egg, beaten
½ cup milk
scant 1 cup raspberries
grated rind of 1 lemon
CRUMBLE TOPPING
3 tablespoons pecans or walnuts,
finely chopped
¼ cup dark brown sugar
3 tablespoons all-purpose flour
1 teaspoon ground cinnamon
3 tablespoons butter, melted

MAKES 12

1 Preheat the oven to 350°F. Lightly grease a 12-cup muffin tin, or use paper baking cups. Sift the flour, baking powder and salt into a bowl. Stir in the sugars and cinnamon.

2 Make a well in the center of the flour mixture. Add the butter, egg and milk and mix until just combined. Stir in the raspberries and lemon rind. Divide the mixture among the muffin cups.

3 Make the crumble topping by mixing the nuts, dark brown sugar, flour and cinnamon in a bowl. Add the melted butter and stir to blend. Spoon some of the crumble over each uncooked muffin. Bake for 20–25 minutes, or until the muffins are well risen and golden brown. Let cool on a wire rack, then pack in a tin.

54

Dried Fruit Tea Bread

INGREDIENTS

1 cup dried fruit, roughly chopped
1 cup hot tea
2 cups whole-wheat self-rising flour
1 teaspoon grated nutmeg
¼ cup dark brown sugar
3 tablespoons sunflower oil
3 tablespoons skim milk
raw sugar, for sprinkling

SERVES 8–10

55

1 Soak the chopped dried fruit in the hot tea for several hours or overnight, making sure the fruit is completely covered. Drain and reserve both the fruit and the liquid.

2 Preheat the oven to 350°F. Grease a 7-inch round cake pan and line the bottom with parchment paper. Be sure to grease the paper well.

3 Sift the flour into a large bowl with the grated nutmeg. Stir in the brown sugar, fruit and tea. Add the sunflower oil and skim milk and mix well.

4 Spoon the mixture into the prepared pan and sprinkle with raw sugar. Bake for 50–55 minutes or until the mixture is just firm. Cool on a wire rack, then cut into thick chunks and pack in a tin.

Biscotti

INGREDIENTS

4 tablespoons unsalted butter, softened
½ cup superfine sugar
1½ cups self-rising flour
¼ teaspoon salt
2 teaspoons baking powder
1 teaspoon ground coriander
finely grated rind of 1 lemon
¼ cup polenta
1 egg, lightly beaten
2 teaspoons brandy or orange liqueur
¼ cup pistachios

MAKES 24

1 Preheat the oven to 325°F. Lightly grease a baking sheet. In a mixing bowl, cream the butter with the sugar until the mixture is light and fluffy.

2 Sift the flour, salt, baking powder and coriander into the mixing bowl. Add the lemon rind, polenta, egg and brandy. Mix to a soft dough.

3 Work in the nuts until they are evenly distributed. Halve the mixture and then shape each half into a sausage shape, about 9 inches long and 2½ inches  in diameter. Place on the baking sheet and bake for about 30 minutes, until risen and just firm. Remove the baking sheet, but leave the oven on.

4 When the loaves are cool, use a serrated knife to cut each of them diagonally into 12 thin slices. Place the slices on the baking sheet, cut side up, and bake for 10 more minutes, until crisp. Cool on a wire rack, then pack in a tin.

COOK'S TIP
These Italian biscuits are traditionally served dipped in a sweet dessert wine - ideal for those who don't have to drive home from the picnic.

Figs with Ricotta Cream

INGREDIENTS

½ cup ricotta cheese
3 tablespoons crème fraîche
1 tablespoon clear honey
½ teaspoon vanilla extract
4 ripe, fresh figs
grated nutmeg, to decorate

SERVES 4

1 Mix the ricotta cheese, crème fraîche, honey and vanilla in a bowl. Transfer to a container with a tight-fitting lid and pack in a cooler with the figs. Pack a nutmeg – and a nutmeg grater – if you really want to impress.

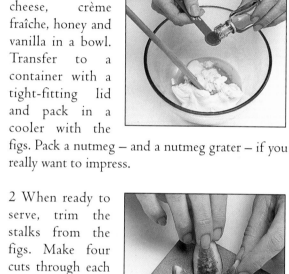

2 When ready to serve, trim the stalks from the figs. Make four cuts through each fig from the stalk end, cutting them almost through but leaving them joined at the base. Place each fig on an individual plate and open it out like a flower.

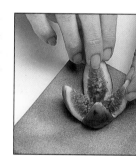

3 Spoon a little ricotta cream onto each plate and grate nutmeg on top to serve.

VARIATION

Use low-fat cream cheese instead of ricotta, if desired, and substitute plain yogurt for the crème fraîche. Sprinkle the yogurt with raw sugar.

Chocolate Chip Banana Crêpes

INGREDIENTS

2 ripe bananas
scant 1 cup milk
2 eggs
1 1/4 cups self-rising flour
1/3 cup ground almonds
1 tablespoon superfine sugar
3 tablespoons chocolate chips
butter for frying
TOPPING
2/3 cup heavy cream
1 tablespoon confectioners' sugar
toasted sliced almonds

MAKES 16

1 Mash the bananas in a bowl with a fork. Stir in half the milk, then beat in the eggs. Gradually beat in the flour, ground almonds and superfine sugar. Make a well in the center of the mixture and pour in the remaining milk. Add the chocolate chips and stir to make a thick batter.

2 Heat a pat of butter in a nonstick frying pan. Spoon in a little of the batter so that it spreads to form a small crêpe. Make more crêpes in the same way, but do not overcrowd the pan.

3 When bubbles appear on the tops of the crêpes, turn them over and briefly cook the other side. Cool on a wire rack, then pack in a tin.

4 For the topping, either whip the cream with the confectioners' sugar and pack in a plastic container in a cooler, or cheat and use canned whipped cream. Pack the toasted almonds separately, to decorate the crêpes.

59

COOK'S TIP

The easiest way to cook these crêpes is in an electric frying pan, if you have one. Children enjoy making them (with adult help), especially if they are allowed to use the chocolate chips to make faces on the crêpes.

Orange-blossom Jelly

INGREDIENTS

5 tablespoons superfine sugar
⅔ cup water
2 tablespoons powdered gelatin
2½ cups freshly squeezed orange juice
2 tablespoons orange-flower water

SERVES 4–6

60

I Place the superfine sugar and water in a small saucepan. Heat gently, stirring occasionally, until the sugar has dissolved. Transfer to a heatproof bowl and sprinkle in the gelatin. Let stand until the gelatin has absorbed the liquid and is solid.

2 Melt the gelatin again by placing the bowl over a pan of gently simmering water. When it is clear, remove it from the heat. Let the gelatin cool, but do not let it solidify. Stir it into the orange juice and add the orange-flower water.

3 Wet a ring mold, pour in the orange jelly and chill in the refrigerator for at least 3 hours, until solidly set. Turn the jelly out by immersing the mold in a bowl of hot water. Return the jelly to the mold, wrap it carefully and place it in a cooler to transport to the picnic. Turn the jelly out to serve; for a special occasion, decorate with fresh flowers. Serve with dessert biscuits such as langues de chat, if desired.

COOK'S TIP
The acid in orange juice inhibits the setting action of gelatin, which is why the quantity in this recipe is relatively high. It is important to cool the liquid gelatin before adding it to the orange juice, or it will form threads.

Pear & Almond Cream Tart

INGREDIENTS

*¾ pound shortcrust or sweet
shortcrust pastry*
3 firm pears
lemon juice
1 tablespoon peach brandy or water
¼ cup peach preserves, strained
ALMOND CREAM FILLING
5 tablespoons butter
¼ cup superfine sugar
¾ cup ground almonds
1 egg, plus 1 egg white
few drops of almond extract

SERVES 6

1 Preheat the oven to 375°F. Roll out the pastry on a lightly floured surface and use it to line a 9-inch tart pan. Make the almond cream filling by creaming the butter with the sugar in a small bowl, then stirring in the ground almonds, egg, egg white and almond extract.

2 Peel the pears, cut them in half and remove the cores. Brush with lemon juice to prevent them from turning brown. With the rounded sides up, slice the pears thinly crosswise, keeping the slices together.

3 Spoon the almond cream filling into the uncooked pastry shell. Slide a spatula under each pear in turn, gently pressing the top to fan out the slices, and transfer it to the pastry shell. Arrange the pear slices like the spokes of a wheel. Bake the tart for 50–55 minutes or until the filling is set and golden brown. Cool on a wire rack.

4 Meanwhile, heat the brandy with the peach preserves in a small pan, then brush the mixture over the top of the hot tart to glaze. Let sit until quite cool, then wrap carefully and transport to the picnic in a rigid box.

Index